HOPE IN THE EVERLASTING

Advent

25 Days Devotional

Readings for a Christmas Season
of Countercultural Joy and Deep Hope.

FANI REYES DE JESÚS

Disciplinas
LIBERTADORAS

Editor: Hector De Jesús Jr.
Cover and interior design: Fani Reyes De Jesús
Disciplinas Libertadoras' Ministry, Inc. endorses the author.
Visit the ministry at: www.facebook.com/disciplinaslibertadoras

ISBN: 979-8-9894690-1-7 (Paperback)
Subjects: Advent | Christian Life | Religion | Holiday

Printed in the United States of America

THERE IS HOPE IN THE EVERLASTING!

To:

_____

From:

_____

*For all who seek truth and long to experience
the countercultural joy and hope
that comes with the birth of Christ.*

*This edition is in honor of
my late spiritual mother and mentor,
Dr. Daisy Quintana,
who imprinted on my soul
the hope in the everlasting.*

Contents

Embracing Advent

WHY DO WE NEED ADVENT?

The Advent season was unfamiliar to me. During my childhood, the Christmas season revolved around family gatherings, traditional foods, Christmas carols, and the anticipation of Three Kings' Day. As I grew older and began embracing Christianity and discovering the true meaning of Christmas, the season then started to revolve around social, familial, and religious pressures and expectations: What gifts to give? Whom to visit? Which traditions to honor? Which church activities to attend? Which friends could I celebrate with without compromising my convictions? The season's endless demands and social pressures became overwhelming, stealing all the joy during the "most joyful time of the year."

In the weeks leading up to Christmas, pausing to reflect on Jesus' birth and its impact on my eternity was pushed aside until December 24. When Christmas Eve arrived, a sense of emptiness filled my soul, and the awareness of my neglect made me realize: I had lost sight of what mattered most. By then, the guilt of being swept up by pressures, busyness, culture, and society brought me shame, and Christmas Day would come and go without the reflection it deserved.

I'm not alone in this experience. Like me, many people spend much of the Christmas season submerged in cultural traditions and trying to meet the expectations of their social circles. On the other hand, in our faith traditions, we may fill our schedules with church activities meant to commemorate the birth of Christ. Yet, we end up in the same place—without a deep, personal appreciation for what this season truly signifies.

As Christmas approached each year, it was always the same: an emotional struggle between the anticipation of celebrating Christ's birth and the crushing pressure of meeting the season's demands. One year, I discovered that other Christian communities intentionally set apart the weeks before Christmas to escape this struggle through a personal Advent journey. Because of the season's many demands, Advent invites us to pause and find a balance between schedules weighed down by traditions and tasks and a genuine appreciation for Christ's coming.

MY EXPERIENCE WITH ADVENT

One year, I joined a friend's church program during Advent, and this practice completely changed my perspective, focus, and way of preparing for the Christmas celebration. I still enjoy decorating my home, giving gifts, visiting my loved ones, and listening to Christmas carols, but these activities are no longer my priority, nor do they consume my thoughts and time as they once did.

That experience marked a turning point in my commemorating Jesus' initial arrival on earth and in my personal life. I had finally found an antidote to my annual struggle!

The term "Advent" comes from the Latin "adventus," meaning "coming" or "arrival." In Christianity, it refers to a period that begins four weeks before Christmas Day, during which believers prepare to commemorate the initial arrival of Jesus at His birth. This preparation involves turning their minds and hearts to the person and work of Jesus, reflecting on His deeds with fervent anticipation and expectation for the Advent of His second coming—His eventual return for them.

Advent allows me to enjoy beautiful traditions and magical decorations without letting them overshadow the immense joy and wonder of celebrating the birth that transformed history and the destiny of humanity. No matter how magical and moving they may be, the decorations, traditions, and so on can never fill my soul like the moments with Christ that Advent offers me.

I have turned Advent into a preventive mechanism to avoid getting lost in the noise or being caught up by the pressures of the season and to remember the real reason for the celebration: the birth of the Savior of the world, and on a personal level, the Savior of my soul.

Over time, I have understood that even though Advent may not be the trend of the world or the most popular way to celebrate Christmas, deviating from culture and what is popular is always beneficial when anchoring my hope in eternity. Every year, Advent reminds me that during those four weeks leading up to December 25, there should be nothing more important in my heart. While this may seem obvious to those with Christian faith, and we might loudly proclaim, "Of course! Nothing is more important than Jesus during this time," the lack of balance between cultural traditions, commercial hustle, and spiritual reflection assails us each year and tends to rob us of the true hope that Christmas brings to our lives.

WHY THIS DEVOTIONAL?

One year, a friend invited me to participate in Advent for the first time; I often wished I had discovered it earlier. It would have saved me many emotional and spiritual struggles. Battling these sorts of feelings alone has never been easy, and finding tools that help me experience the victory of living free from the accusations of a deceitful heart and a constant enemy of the soul, makes me feel a responsibility to share what I've discovered, hoping to lighten the burdens of others.

One of Satan's great weapons is to make us believe that we live in isolation. With this deceptive lie, he often manages to corner us into living in a dark world where the shame of our human struggles prompts us to pretend we are living in hope when, in reality, we find ourselves hopeless and in a broken inner world. With this devotional, I do not intend to change your life but rather to let you know that you are not the only person who has navigated the holiday season between joys and sorrows.

I desire to inspire you to be intentional and to discover that despite the pressures culture and traditions throw at us, we hold the key to experiencing Christmas with the right hope. Enjoying our traditions is beautiful, but when they take an inappropriate place, they can rob us of the fullness that only Jesus can provide.

A second reason for this devotional is this reality: we are prone to forget! Not just at Christmas but throughout the year what the arrival of Christ has done for us. Therefore, with this devotional, I aim to saturate our minds with not just my experiences but also with transcendent scriptural truths that will anchor our spirits, helping us remember His glorious salvation and the everlasting hope we have beyond December 25.

HOW TO USE THIS DEVOTIONAL?

Your personal Advent journey will begin on December 1. You will find a daily devotional reading that will help you pause and absorb the wonder of the season through accounts of Christ's birth, His work, and the promises brought forth by His arrival.

You will find personal reflection questions at the end of each reading that will help you make room for hope as you trade the pressures and struggles of the season for the hope Christ's birth brought to us. As you reflect on your answers, set aside any shame, be honest with what is in your heart, and allow Jesus to meet you in your responses.

I encourage you to share your experiences during this journey with others in your celebration circle.

This devotional invites you to celebrate Christmas differently, helping you overcome distractions and savor the wonder of Jesus' birth above the pressures, emotions, and fleeting traditions.

Joined with you in this season of joy and hope,
Fani

Introduction

EMBRACING ETERNAL HOPE

For many, Christmas is the most anticipated season of the year. It's a magical time filled with bright lights, cherished traditions, and memories that fill our hearts with joy and expectation. However, I can affirm from experience that there can be many reasons to feel discouraged during the holiday season. The circumstances of the world, the weight of sin, financial struggles, the absence of a family member, seemingly unsolvable problems, and broken relationships are some situations that can leave us feeling hopeless as we enter this season.

Nevertheless, the meaning behind the birth we commemorate makes this time of year genuinely hopeful. The birth of Jesus marked not just a Christmas day but the beginning of the story of redemption for all humanity. This season fills us with living hope because it reminds us that one day, there will be an Advent: the child born in a humble manger will return for us, and with His return, all affliction, hopelessness, and pain will vanish for those who have made space in their hearts for Him.

Christmas serves as a reminder that the birth of Jesus brought a hope that is not fleeting, like our circumstances or the days of

December, but eternal and transcending of the most significant challenges we might face.

The promise of Advent fills us with hope that goes beyond festivities and material gifts. It connects us to the promise of eternal life, where redemption, peace, and abundance will be a constant reality. The return of Jesus inspires us to embrace the hope of a better world.

Hope of peace! Hope of love! Hope of redemption! The hope of eternity! How do we embrace this hope? Embracing eternal hope requires us to cultivate a deep connection with our faith and keep it present daily. The Advent season allows us to do just that. It is a personal journey in which you choose to pause and enjoy Christmas by taking moments for reflection and individual worship, rekindling your awe for Jesus' birth's profound significance for your eternity.

In the coming days, you will be challenged to find a balance between the traditional festivities of the season and your connection to the one thing that can keep your hope steadfast. You will embrace eternal hope as you remember that authentic joy in our lives does not depend on circumstances, festivities, or cultural and social commerce but springs from the knowledge that the true hope we need is anchored and rooted in eternity.

Make this season a spark to ignite the flame of your hope. As you dedicate time to daily reflection, you will nurture your joy beyond the festive agenda and embrace the genuine hope that Jesus' birth brings, one reflection at a time.

The people who walk in darkness will see a great light. The light will shine on those living in the land of dark shadows.
Isaiah 9:2

Day 1

And he will turn many of the children of Israel to the Lord their God. He will also go before Him in the spirit and power of Elijah, 'to turn the hearts of the fathers to the children,' and the disobedient to the wisdom of the just, to make ready a people prepared for the Lord.

Luke 1: 16 - 17

Day 1

LET US PREPARE A DWELLING

In today's passage, we find the remarkable work of John the Baptist, whose purpose was to prepare the way for the arrival of the Messiah and turn rebellious hearts back to their Lord God. From the wilderness, with an urgent voice, he called many to repentance, proclaiming the imminent coming of Christ and the need for the people to be rightly prepared for His arrival.

This call was for the people of that time and us today in this season.

At times, I have needed help to respond to this call. While my heart longs to be a worthy place for Christ's presence, I must admit that I sometimes falter. There are moments when fleeting desires, quick fixes, and temporary remedies draw me. Yet, at the end of all these paths, a persistent emptiness reminds me that my heart finds true fulfillment only when I give Christ the place He deserves.

I'm sure I'm not alone in this struggle. Have you felt the same?

With its magic, excitement, and festive spirit, the Christmas season often makes us prone to neglecting the need to prepare our hearts for Christ. We might be tempted to confine His presence to a small corner beneath the Christmas tree this season. However, just as John the Baptist fervently urged hearts to prepare for the coming of the Messiah, we too must begin this season sensing the urgent need to turn our hearts and make room for Jesus in our celebrations. Let us take heed: the transient joy of festive decorations, social gatherings, and gift shopping can leave us with hearts unprepared and devoid of space for the Son of God.

Before you're fully immersed in holiday preparations, I'd like you to start this Advent season by responding to this call. Setting aside space for Christ in our hearts will require your intention during Advent. Turn your heart to God and seek wisdom. Make it a goal to smooth the way for the Messiah's arrival through personal reflection that helps you understand His work in your life. Lastly, prepare your heart to go beyond traditions and social expectations; let everything you do in your preparations reflect the proper commemoration He deserves.

Please ensure that everything you plan during these festive days includes space for Him in your life and your family. If you do, He will genuinely dwell in your heart, and you'll be better prepared to receive Him at His glorious return.

My dwelling place will be with them;
I will be their God, and they will be my people.
Ezekiel 37:27

Create Room for Hope: A Time to Reflect

*Can you identify the place Jesus holds in your heart
as this season begins?*

Where is your focus directed this Christmas?

What place does Christ's return hold amid your preparations?

*What actions can you take to focus your heart and
lean towards Jesus in the coming days?*

*I will give them a heart to know me, that I am the Lord.
They will be my people, and I will be their God,
for they will return to me with all their heart.*
Jeremiah 24:7

Day 2

*But the angel said to him: "Do not be afraid,
Zechariah; your prayer has been heard. Your wife
Elizabeth will bear you a son, and you are to call him
John. . . Zechariah asked the angel, "How can I be sure
of this? I am an old man and my wife is well along in
years." The angel said to him, "I am Gabriel. I stand
in the presence of God, and I have been sent to speak
to you and to tell you this good news."*

Luke 1: 13 - 14 ; 18 - 19

Day 2

A MARVELOUS MIRACLE

In the Gospel of Luke, we find the story of a priest named Zechariah. He and his wife, Elizabeth, had never had children and were now advanced in years. For years, they had prayed for a child to carry on their legacy, but with their age, it seemed unlikely their request would ever be granted.

One day, while Zechariah was serving in the temple, it appeared that God had finally remembered his prayer—though, in truth, it was simply God's perfect timing; everything was unfolding according to His plan. An angel arrived to announce the great miracle they were to receive: Zechariah and his wife would have a son. Yet, Zechariah's circumstances and age led him to confusion and deep doubt when faced with this incredible revelation. Even so, God remained faithful to His promise, and Zechariah and Elizabeth conceived John the Baptist, the forerunner of the Messiah.

As Zechariah encountered the miracle he had prayed for so fervently, his human frailty overcame him, and his faith wavered. He began to see his circumstances as too great an obstacle for God. Sometimes, we also feel this way. When we look at our reality, we may be tempted to focus on our circumstances and doubt that God can work miracles on our behalf.

The birth of this miraculous son was not only a gift to an elderly couple but also a testimony to God's power and faithfulness.

The most astounding miracle that God has ever performed in our favor was fulfilling His promise of redemption through the gift of His Son, Jesus.

During this season, as we prepare to celebrate the miracle of Jesus' birth, let us open our hearts to hope by placing our confidence in God's power and faithfulness. To fully embrace the wonder and joy of the Christmas season, we must fill our minds with the marvels of what God has done and continues to do in our lives.

Perhaps you, like Zechariah, have long prayed for an unanswered miracle and feel your hope slipping away. As you move through this season, remember that what fills our hearts goes beyond what we have or think we lack. Hold to this truth: the birth of Christ will always fill us more than any miracle we could ask for or imagine.

Embrace the hope of this season, knowing that the greatest miracle Zechariah received was not simply a son but the announcement of the good news of redemption for the world.

Now to him who is able to do immeasurably more
than all we ask or imagine, according to his power
that is at work within us.
Ephesians 3:20

Create Room for Hope: A Time to Reflect

*Have you experienced moments when you prayed for
a miracle and it seemed there was no answer?
How did you feel during those times?*

*What does it mean to you that what fills your heart goes
beyond what you have or think you lack?*

*How can you embrace hope this Christmas season by internalizing
the truth that Christ's birth is the greatest miracle we have
received and the only gift that fills us beyond anything
we could ask for or desire?*

Not one of all the Lord's good promises
to Israel failed; every one was fulfilled.
Joshua 21:45

Day 3

And Mary said:
"My soul glorifies the Lord and my spirit rejoices in God my Savior, for he has been mindful of the humble state of his servant. From now on all generations will call me blessed, for the Mighty One has done great things for me—holy is his name. His mercy extends to those who fear him, from generation to generation."

Luke 1: 46 - 50

Day 3

DIVINE SALVATION

"Save yourselves!" is a phrase I've heard since childhood, used to denote a chaotic situation and urge people to run for their lives to avoid imminent harm. This idea of "save yourselves" has become a norm in our current world. But when it comes to sin, the truth is that no matter what measures we take, we cannot save ourselves.

In today's passage, we find Mary, the mother of Jesus, just after receiving the news that she is carrying the Savior of the world in her womb. According to Jewish law, Mary's physical life was at risk due to her out-of-wedlock pregnancy. But Mary also seems to have understood that her spiritual life was in even greater imminent danger. Mary needed a divine Savior to save her; her song reveals that she fully understood this. Can you imagine receiving the news that Mary did? *Mary, your Savior has come—and is growing in your womb!* How would you react?

Upon hearing the divine nature of her pregnancy, a song of praise burst from her lips. Genuine worship poured out from her heart as Mary instantly magnified the Lord. Her praise was likely interrupted by her questions amid her circumstances. Still, her words show that, in that moment, she understood that the Savior she desperately needed was closer than ever.

This Advent season reminds us that the world of Mary's days and our world today is the same, still in a fallen state, and therefore, we desperately need someone to save us from the imminent danger threatening our souls. Contrary to what society urges us to do daily, we cannot save ourselves. Like Mary, we all need a divine Savior. Regarding our spiritual lives, saving ourselves doesn't apply. Sin has touched each of us, and we struggle with it daily. Our efforts to protect ourselves from the dangers threatening our souls are futile and hopeless.

But amid this spiritual chaos comes Christmas—the moment we celebrate the birth of the Savior of the world, Jesus Christ. Jesus is the fulfillment of humanity's divine hope. His coming offers us the salvation we so desperately need.

During this season, let's remember that Jesus is the Savior who has come to rescue us from the danger of sin and offer us eternal life. So, instead of scrambling to save ourselves, we can rest in the Savior God has provided through Jesus Christ.

Christmas reminds us that God has intervened in our spiritual chaos by offering us the only redemption and hope that can save our souls. Today, let us sing with hope. We have been rescued and filled with eternal hope, which calls for a song of praise—our most sincere praise!

Salvation is found in no one else,
for there is no other name under heaven given to
mankind by which we must be saved.
Acts 4:12

Create Room for Hope: A Time to Reflect

Have you ever felt trapped in a spiritually dangerous situation and looking for a way to save yourself?

How do you feel when you rest in the Savior God provided in Jesus Christ? How near do you think His salvation and favor towards you?

Can you join Mary in her song with a song of your own? What would your song say if you were to write a song of praise like hers?

I will rejoice in the Lord!
I will be joyful in the God of my salvation!
Habakkuk 3:18

Day 4

Blessed is the Lord God of Israel,
For He has visited and redeemed His people,
And has raised up a horn of salvation for us
In the house of His servant David,
As He spoke by the mouth of His holy prophets,
Who have been since the world began.

Luke 1: 68 - 70

Day 4

COMPLETE REDEMPTION

There is a significant difference between being saved and being redeemed. Salvation freed us from the danger of sin and death. But redemption is the price paid by Christ's life so that sin and shame would no longer have any hold over our conscience.

In our world, redemption can sometimes feel incomplete. When confronted with the accusations of sin, it's difficult to fully rest in the truth that Christ has paid the price in full. But it's a fact—He did. No matter how much we may want to add to our redemption with our efforts, it doesn't change the reality that Christ's payment covered the entire amount owed. A clean slate was granted to us through the birth of the Son of our redeeming God.

In today's reading, Zechariah's prophecy of visitation and redemption for Israel pointed to the fulfillment of a promise that the people had awaited with great hope. But when the promise arrived, it felt incomplete. The prophecies of how redemption would come began to be fulfilled with the arrival of Jesus on the day of His birth. Yet, for some, His redemption lacked the possessions, wealth, and honor they expected from a mighty Savior.

We often experience the same struggle. We question the effectiveness of Christ's redemption, comparing His payment to the depths of our sins and wrongdoings. We look at our past in light of Christ's redemptive payment and think, "There's no way His redemption fully covers my debt." But it does! Not only did He pay the price, but He encouraged us through His Word to let go of our shame and to see ourselves through Him.

The birth, death, and resurrection of Jesus fulfilled the necessary payment for our redemption, and nothing we do can diminish its eternal nature once we accept Him as our Savior.

This is a gift we can unwrap—not just at Christmas, but time and time again—each time the enemy accuses us and leads us to guilt, making us feel and believe that our debt remains unsettled. In the midst of our limited understanding of redemption, let us celebrate Christmas with this knowledge: the birth of Jesus was the beginning of a work that fully paid for our sins and shame.

For you know that it was not with perishable
things such as silver or gold that you were
redeemed from the empty way of life handed
down to you from your ancestors, but with the
precious blood of Christ, a lamb without
blemish or defect.
1 Peter 1:18-19

Create Room for Hope: A Time to Reflect

How complete has Christ's redemption become for you?

Do you wrestle with any accusation that makes you feel you need to pay a higher price than He already paid for your wrongdoings? How can you "unwrap" His gift of redemption over that accusation?

How does knowing that the redemption of your sins is complete and eternal help you celebrate this season in a different way?

For he has rescued us from the dominion of darkness and brought us into the kingdom of the Son he loves, in whom we have redemption, the forgiveness of sins.
Colossians 1:13-14

Day 5

And it came to pass in those days that a decree went out from Caesar Augustus that all the world should be registered. This census first took place while Quirinius was governing Syria. So all went to be registered, everyone to his own city. Joseph also went up from Galilee, out of the city of Nazareth, into Judea, to the city of David, which is called Bethlehem, because he was of the house and lineage of David, to be registered with Mary, his betrothed wife, who was with child.

Luke 2:1-5

Day 5

SUPREME AND SOVEREIGN GOD

The story of Jesus' birth began during the reign of one of the most notable men of ancient history—the ruler of Rome, Caesar Augustus. For years, Caesar Augustus fought for control, driven by his desire to become Emperor of the Roman Empire, and he had finally achieved it. As a result of years of battles for power, the world into which Jesus was to be born lay in ruins and fragments. With a hidden plan, God began moving pieces to reveal who held supreme authority. God used Caesar's rule in His sovereignty to introduce His divine order through a historic act: executing the first census.

This historical background may, at first glance, seem irrelevant to the Christmas story of Jesus' birth, but it is far from it. This census remarkably marks the sovereignty of God. God used an invincible monarch to fulfill His plan and divine will. Caesar Augustus' decree made all of Rome aware of the birth of a child, unlike any other. This census, so meticulously orchestrated by a sovereign God, ensured that the birth of this divinely conceived child would be recorded in a dominant empire's historical records—highlighting events that pointed to a supreme divinity reigning above all and overall.

God's sovereignty is supreme. His reign is like no other, and knowing that we serve a sovereign God in our fragmented world changes everything. It transforms the assurance and confidence with which we celebrate the commemoration of Jesus' birth. The fact that God exercised His sovereignty over the most powerful empire of the time, using Caesar to announce His arrival, is a trustworthy testimony that He remains sovereign today—over us, our circumstances, our future, our culture, and our society.

God's sovereignty, evident in the story of Jesus' birth, is an unchanging reminder that He controls every aspect of our existence and life. Throughout this year, we may have experienced significant fragmentation. Amid apparent losses, ruins, and struggles against powers of this age, you may not have noticed the census God has enacted in your life to highlight His sovereignty.

During this Advent season, I encourage you to take an inventory—a census of all you've lived through this year. Can you trace His plan through your fragmented world? God's sovereignty over every stage we live through reminds us that His good news for us can never be altered.

All the peoples of the earth are regarded as nothing.
He does as he pleases with the powers of heaven
and the peoples of the earth. No one can hold
back his hand or say to him: "What have you done?"
Daniel 4:35

Create Room for Hope: A Time to Reflect

*What emotions do you evoke when considering
God's sovereignty amid your current circumstances?*

*What does God's supremacy mean to you in this season?
Are there areas where you need to remember God's sovereignty?*

*How does knowing that God used Caesar's government as part of His
plan to highlight His supremacy help you trust that everything you
are experiencing serves to emphasize His sovereignty in your life?*

And we know that in all things God works for
the good of those who love him, who have been
called according to his purpose.
Romans 8:28

Day 6

So it was, that while they were there, the days were completed for her to be delivered. And she brought forth her firstborn Son, and wrapped Him in swaddling cloths, and laid Him in a manger, because there was no room for them in the inn.

Luke 2: 6 - 7

Day 6

PROVISION FOR SCARCE SOULS

Places of scarcity terrify us. Scarcity reminds us that we are deprived of something we desire or need. No one in their right mind would choose to leave the comfort of abundance for a place where only uncertainty awaits—except for Jesus.

In the narrative of His birth, as told in the Gospel of Luke, we witness the Divine God, the owner of the universe, being born in the most humble conditions: a stable in the small town of Bethlehem. There were no comforts, only swaddling clothes and the arms of His mother to embrace Him, stripped of all His glory and wealth.

I can imagine Mary's heart in the face of the scarcity surrounding her first experience of motherhood, especially when I compare her situation to the lavish preparations I've seen my friends make for the arrival of their babies: beautifully decorated nurseries, carefully arranged cribs, and wardrobes overflowing with clothes. Certainly, a stable and a manger were not what Mary envisioned for the birth of her first child. I have no doubt that, in addition to feeling terrified, she also felt sorrow at the scarcity around her. But this, too, was part of God's plan. By offering redemption to all of humanity yet having no place to lay His head, Jesus shows us that His divine provision is not limited by scarcity.

The birth of Christ in a place of scarcity powerfully emphasizes that God's provision could often come from the least expected places and in the most humble circumstances.

During this Advent season, let us regain our awe at God's provision. Often, we define God's provision as the absence of scarcity, abundant satisfaction, and fulfilled desires. But the place of Jesus' birth teaches us that accurate provision consists of receiving what we truly need when we need it most.

Material scarcity in our lives cannot compare to the scarcity sin has caused in our souls. But with His birth, Jesus made a divine provision that has removed this lack. His coming gave us a continuous source of provision to satisfy our lives where we are most lacking. If we look at our shortcomings in light of the divine provision He has made for our scarce souls, the places of scarcity will not hinder us from anchoring our contentment in the fullness that Jesus came to provide.

In the Christmas story, Mary may not have had the place she desired most for her child's birth, but amid the scarcity surrounding her, she had what she needed most: the Savior of her soul in her arms.

His divine power has given us everything we need for a godly life through our knowledge of him who called us by his own glory and goodness.
2 Peter 1:3

Create Room for Hope: A Time to Reflect

How do you respond to times of scarcity?
Where in your life have you witnessed divine provision during
moments of need? How has that shaped your perspective?

Considering the material scarcity surrounding the birth of Christ,
can you view scarcity as a chance for God to reveal His divine
provision in your life?

How does your faith in Jesus influence your ability to confront and rise
above challenges related to both material and spiritual scarcity?

The young lions lack and suffer hunger;
But those who seek the Lord
shall not lack any good thing.
Psalm 34:10

Day 7

Now there were in the same country shepherds living out in the fields, keeping watch over their flock by night. And behold, an angel of the Lord stood before them, and the glory of the Lord shone around them, and they were greatly afraid. Then the angel said to them, "Do not be afraid, for behold, I bring you good tidings of great joy which will be to all people.

Luke 2: 8 - 10

Day 7

DIVINE ENCOUNTER

Can you recall a memorable encounter you've had with someone? Christmas is full of reunions with loved ones—some we haven't seen in a long time and others who, despite being nearby, we don't get to visit as often due to life's responsibilities. The holiday season seems to add hours to our schedules magically. The thrilling desire to embrace each other and celebrate together prompts us to find creative ways to plan gatherings.

In today's reading, we find an encounter between angels and shepherds that undoubtedly changed their plans and the course of history itself. In the darkness of night, angels wrapped in glory descended from the heavens. With a mission marked by the gospel announcement, they appeared to a group of marginalized men watching over their flocks.

This was not a traditional Christmas gathering among family and friends. There were no festive dishes or wrapped gifts. The excitement of this encounter was heightened by the message behind this proclamation: *"I bring you good news of great joy that will be for all the people."* The radiant glory accompanying this announcement was a fitting backdrop for such excellent news of salvation.

What is genuinely divine about this encounter is that, during those times, society tended to overlook shepherds. They were not only disregarded for what was considered their lowly work but were also considered untrustworthy. It's no wonder they were afraid upon seeing that brilliant light. Yet, it was precisely with them that God scheduled this encounter to announce the birth of His Divine Son and Savior on the night He was born. This encounter between the shepherds and the voice of the Creator reassured them that, despite their marginalized status, they were included in God's plan of salvation. What a wonderful gesture from God towards them!

The birth of Jesus on that night brought good news of great joy for all creation. This good news includes you and me, regardless of our social status, marginalized places, or past and current circumstances.

This Advent season encourages us to make time for a meaningful encounter with the God of our salvation—not to dwell in fear or self-condemnation, but to rekindle our awe for His everlasting redemption.

So that they should seek the Lord, in the hope
that they might grope for Him and find Him,
though He is not far from each one of us.
Acts 17:27

Create Room for Hope: A Time to Reflect

How do you usually celebrate Christmas gatherings with your loved ones?
What special significance do these moments hold for you?

Reflect on the message of the angels to the shepherds:
"I bring you good news that will cause great joy for all the people."
What does this good news mean to you personally?

What is the significance of God choosing the shepherds,
often marginalized, to announce the birth of His Son?
What lesson can you draw from this choice?

For those who find me find life
and receive favor from the Lord.
Proverbs 8:35

Day 8

This will be a sign to you:
You will find a baby wrapped in cloths and lying in
a manger. Suddenly a great company of the heavenly
host appeared with the angel, praising God and
saying, "Glory to God in the highest heaven, and on
earth peace to those on whom his favor rests."

Luke 2: 12 - 14

Day 8

HE IS OUR PEACE

Christmas does not bring peace and hope for everyone. In fact, for many people, the holiday season is marked by nostalgic moments and sad memories, leaving a deep emptiness of hope. Have you ever felt this way? I have. I have gone through times and festive seasons filled with melancholy and a lack of happiness —confused by having it all yet feeling like I have nothing. Due to my own experiences, I wouldn't want to minimize the emotions that arise from missing a loved one who no longer sits at our table or from facing loneliness, financial pressures, unmet expectations, and health struggles. Any of these challenges can undoubtedly overshadow our Christmas traditions and celebrations.

Amid sadness and nostalgia, the birth of Christ brings a peace that surpasses human understanding. It is a peace that does not come from the temporary distractions the world urges us to embrace during this season. This peace, anchored in the divine source of joy that Jesus is, renews and strengthens us, allowing us to face the missing pieces of our lives with serenity and hope.

The joy, peace, and hope we long for are found in Christ, not in earthly things. These joys do not stem from material possessions but from our experiences with Him and in Him.

Festivities, memories of our loved ones, traditions, and gifts aren't inherently bad, but they are broken fountains that can only offer fleeting moments of happiness.

Therefore, we face a significant challenge amid the legitimate emotions and feelings that may visit us during this season. We can allow ourselves to be swayed by societal pressures, seeking peace in various distractions and broken fountains that will consequently fill our hearts with anguish in the days ahead. Or we can bring everything that causes our hearts to ache and disturbs our minds in prayer to the cross that the Son of God bore in exchange for complete peace and leave it there.

In the midst of life's darkness, He remains the source of inexplicable and eternal peace. The birth of Christ on that special Christmas night serves as a powerful reminder that the peace surpassing all understanding is available to those who believe in Him.

This Christmas, may you discover in Christ the true source of our peace and hope.

And the peace of God, which surpasses all
understanding, will guard your hearts
and minds through Christ Jesus.
Philippians 4:7

Create Room for Hope: A Time to Reflect

Have you ever felt sadness or a sense of emptiness during the holiday season? How have you managed those feelings?

How often do you look for joy, peace, and hope in temporary, worldly things during this time? What insights have you gained about how long that joy truly lasts?

In what ways can you connect with the true source of peace and hope that Christ is this Christmas and throughout your life?

Peace I leave with you; my peace I give you.
I do not give to you as the world gives.
Do not let your hearts be troubled and
do not be afraid.
John 14:27

Day 9

When the angels had left them and gone into heaven,
the shepherds said to one another, "Let's go to
Bethlehem and see this thing that has happened,
which the Lord has told us about." So they hurried
off and found Mary and Joseph, and the baby, who
was lying in the manger. When they had seen him,
they spread the word concerning what had been told
them about this child, and all who heard it were
amazed at what the shepherds said to them.

Luke 2: 15 - 18

Day 9

FINDING JESUS IN THE ORDINARY

The angels' announcement was not something the shepherds could overlook. They were filled with an irresistible anticipation and a strong desire to witness everything the angels had proclaimed, hurrying to Bethlehem in search of the promised child.

What a kind gift it is that, despite Jesus being born so many years ago, we can still find Him today. We don't find Him in a manger or wrapped in swaddling clothes; He is present with us daily.

In our pursuit of a deeper relationship with Christ, we sometimes think we must perform spectacular feats or experience extraordinary moments, like angelic manifestations, to be guided to Him. However, because of His birth, finding Jesus today is simpler and more natural than our quest, driven by liturgical and religious acts, might imagine.

Finding Jesus involves inviting Him into our everyday moments—through a text, a phone call, or a short walk. As we wrap gifts and glimpse the lights adorning our city streets and in many other ways, Jesus makes His presence known in our day to day.

How can we see Him? In a whisper that speaks truth to our minds, in the remembrance of a promise, or in a tangible memory of a time we experienced His presence within us.

The presence of Christ in the ordinary manifests through our actions and relationships as we focus on what is transcendent and points us to eternity.

This season, let's not take His presence for granted. Let us be as persistent in finding Him as the shepherds were on the night of His birth. Don't look for Him in a stable, manger, festive moments, or carols. Open your spiritual eyes and discover Him as you carry out your daily life.

In moments when you least expect it, His presence will become palpable. The presence of Jesus does not require rituals or juggling tasks; it is found in our ordinary moments, transforming the mundane of our days into extraordinary experiences.

The Word became flesh and made his dwelling among us. We have seen his glory, the glory of the one and only Son, who came from the Father, full of grace and truth.
John 1:14

Create Room for Hope: A Time to Reflect

How can you be more diligent in seeking Jesus in your daily life?

How can you open your spiritual eyes to become more aware of the divine manifestations of Jesus in your preparations for the season?

What habits or activities might you need to eliminate or reduce in order to pursue Jesus with the same perseverance as the shepherds did?

*I love those who love me,
and those who seek me find me.*
Proverbs 8:17

Day 10

But Mary kept all these things and pondered them in her heart. Then the shepherds returned, glorifying and praising God for all the things that they had heard and seen, as it was told them.

Luke 2: 19 - 20

Day 10

MIXED EMOTIONS

Mary, chosen by God to bring the Savior into the world, experienced a life marked by profound challenges. While this divine selection was indeed honorable, it also came with its share of difficulties and sorrows.

Mary likely became the target of ridicule from many in her town as her pregnancy progressed. She had to leave her home and land, embarking on a long journey without a clear destination. The only certainty Mary probably had was that her future and daily life would be guided by circumstances shrouded in total uncertainty.

During this months-long journey, besides Joseph and her child, Mary's only constant companions were insecurity and profound exhaustion. We cannot overlook that she had left behind her cousin and friend, Elizabeth, who was probably the only person with whom she confided her struggles. She had to give up the companionship of the person capable of understanding her, who listened to her concerns and supported her during this divine assignment. Upon reflection, I have no doubt that the nature of her pregnancy and her announcement of it likely caused her fewer emotions and fears than the challenge of embracing the uncertain world ahead.

As if I were by her side, I can perceive the mixed emotions that Mary must have been experiencing. Her feelings and sense of wonder at God's favor entrusting her with mothering the Savior. Her joy upon receiving her child mixed with anxiety as she listened to what others said about her newborn. Her awe at witnessing the changes her baby boy and Savior were bringing into people's lives. And her mixed emotions at the painful anticipation of having to let her child go when the time came for Him to fulfill His mission of saving the world. Mary must have had many questions and far too few answers.

Today's passage tells us that, upon hearing what others said about her newborn son, Mary treasured all these things and pondered them in her heart. Christmas often brings forth similar feelings as mixed emotions envelop our being, reflecting on our current experiences and the uncertainties ahead.

In the face of an uncertain future filled with mixed emotions, the birth of Christ encourages us to hold in our hearts the things we do not fully understand, trusting in the hope that all these mysteries will one day be revealed.

May your unfailing love be with us, Lord,
even as we put our hope in you.
Psalm 33:22

Create Room for Hope: A Time to Reflect

In what ways do you resonate with Mary?

Can you recall a specific situation or season that has stirred mixed emotions within you, leading you to reflect deeply on your experiences?

How do you think Mary managed her mixed emotions throughout her life, balancing feelings of wonder, sadness, and the anticipation of pain?

How can we incorporate the lesson of cherishing what we don't fully understand into our daily lives, particularly when we encounter uncertainty?

You asked, 'Who is this who hides counsel
without knowledge?' Therefore I have uttered
what I did not understand, things too
wonderful for me, which I did not know.
Job 42:3

Day 11

*And when eight days were completed for the
circumcision of the Child,
His name was called JESUS,
the name given by the angel before
He was conceived in the womb.
Now when the days of her purification
according to the law of Moses were completed,
they brought Him to Jerusalem to
present Him to the Lord.*

Luke 2: 21 - 22

Day 11

JESUS, MORE THAN A NAME

Mary and Joseph named their son Jesus as the angel had instructed. At the time, "Jesus" was a common name, much like John or Joseph today. Yet, from the birth of this divine child, the simplicity of that name transformed into something extraordinary.

After Mary's son was born, the name Jesus ceased to be merely a name called out in streets or households. Because of this child, foretold in the Scriptures, the name Jesus took on a meaning that resonated through history. Jesus became the name spoken in faith by many—young and old, rich and poor, men and women—to affirm promises, offer prayers, and sing praises.

In Hebrew, "Jesus" is Yeshua, meaning "God saves." This became a powerful declaration, a banner that elevated it from just an ordinary name to a Holy one that saved men and women alike.

However, this name took time to unfold its full beauty in my life. For years, I knew Jesus as little more than a religious ritual—a name spoken only in moments of confession, with a sense of fear that I might mispronounce or misstep.

For me, the name of Jesus was to be spoken with reverence, always aware that my sinful lips were too unworthy to call Him endearingly. Yet, over time, as I experienced this name becoming as real as my fears, my relationship with it began to transform. Now, I understand why titles such as Emmanuel, Word, Lamb, and Good Shepherd emerged to describe this exceptional Jesus.

As we prepare to commemorate Christmas and sing hymns and praises with this name, it is both heartening and hopeful to remember that from the birth of the child in the manger, the name Jesus became a refuge and shelter for all those who had been waiting for the Messiah and Savior, generation after generation— and it remains so to this day.

Since that first Christmas, JESUS has been more than a name. The name Jesus became the living testimony that hope and salvation had arrived in this world. Jesus means that we now have salvation, refuge, and hope today and for years and years to come. The name Jesus is more than a name; it is a declaration that salvation has come for you and me.

And His name will be called
Wonderful, Counselor, Mighty God,
Everlasting Father, Prince of Peace.
Isaiah 9:6

Create Room for Hope: A Time to Reflect

How has your perception of the name of Jesus evolved throughout your life? Has Jesus become a cherished name in your personal life?

Have you experienced moments of doubt or fear when mentioning the name of Jesus?

In the context of your current life, what other titles or names might you use to refer to Jesus during this season?

Behold, the virgin shall be with child, and bear a Son, and they shall call His name Immanuel, which is translated, "God with us."
Matthew 1:23

Day 12

And behold, there was a man in Jerusalem whose
name was Simeon, and this man was just and devout,
waiting for the Consolation of Israel, and the Holy
Spirit was upon him. And it had been revealed to him
by the Holy Spirit that he would not see death before
he had seen the Lord's Christ. So he came by the
Spirit into the temple. And when the parents brought
in the Child Jesus, to do for Him according to the
custom of the law, he took Him up in his arms and
blessed God

Luke 2: 25 - 28

Day 12

ROOTED IN HIS PROMISES

In my youth, the anticipation of December—beginning as early as September—marked the start of Christmas gift negotiations with my mother. I was a good student so that I couldn't use grades as my bargaining chip. Instead, I tried other strategies, offering community service hours or dedicating an entire Saturday to cleaning the house, hoping she'd promise me one of my most wished-for gifts. We sealed our agreement with words alone, and I eagerly fulfilled my part, waiting for December 24 to arrive. Curiously, I never asked for a written guarantee; my mother's words instilled in me an unshakable faith that she would keep her promise.

In a world fraught with daily turmoil and decline, we yearn for a steadfast faith in the promises of Jesus—much like the faith I had in those Christmas negotiations with my mother. Faith is the confidence in things unseen yet wholly trusted.

Every day, we need the assurance that the Word is sufficient and that its promises were sealed when Jesus fulfilled His part of the covenant. His coming to earth and paying for humanity's sins through His death carries much more weight of validity than the fulfillment of my mother's words in our Christmas negotiations.

This holds true regardless of what our eyes perceive amidst the constant decline of humanity, morality, and nations.

In today's reading, we encounter a man who did not have to negotiate, as I used to, to ensure he would receive a promise. Simeon was a righteous and devout man, and instead of Christmas gifts, he eagerly awaited the comfort of his people. The Holy Spirit had given him His Word through a revelation: he would see the Counselor before his death. In light of the decline of the people of Israel and the advancement of their oppressors, maintaining faith in that promise became a challenge. Nevertheless, Simeon anchored his faith and hope in the Word that God had given him. When the promise was finally fulfilled, and he held the Counselor in his arms, he praised God. His unshakable faith had been worth it; he was holding the fulfillment of the promise in his hands.

This Advent season reminds us that we don't need to negotiate. Because of Christ's birth, we get to see God's promises fulfilled. Instead, we're challenged to cultivate a steadfast faith that nourishes our conviction that the Word given us will come to pass.

In our own way, Simeon and I witnessed the promises anchored in faith and trust fulfilled. Thanks to Jesus, neither our perceptions nor actions can alter God's Word's certainty. His promises of salvation are faithful, sealed with a resounding "Yes" and "Amen."

God is not a man, that He should lie,
Nor a son of man, that He should repent.
Has He said, and will He not do?
Or has He spoken, and will He not make it good?
Numbers 23:19

Create Room for Hope: A Time to Reflect

What weight do the Words of God hold for you?
Have you ever attempted to negotiate with Him for a favor?

What promise from God can you anchor yourself in?
Even if it seems like its fulfillment is taking too long, remember that
God's promises are "Yes" and "Amen." If you have let go of those
promises, are you willing to revisit them today and re-anchor yourself
in their truth?

In facing the chaos and uncertainty of the current world, how can faith
in these promises serve as a source of comfort for you?

Let us hold fast the confession of our hope without
wavering, for He who promised is faithful.
Hebrews 10:23

Day 13

*Now after Jesus was born in Bethlehem of Judea in
the days of Herod the king, behold,
wise men from the East came to Jerusalem, saying,
"Where is He who has been born King of the Jews?
For we have seen His star in the East
and have come to worship Him."*

Matthew 2: 1 - 2

Day 13

WE WILL FOLLOW THE STAR

During Christmas 2020, Disciplinas Libertadora's ministry's theme was "We Will Follow the Star." We focused our teachings on the story told in today's reading, which recounts the journey of the wise men from the East. These magi, astrologers of royal descent and Gentile origin, embarked on a journey following the radiant light of the star that announced the birth of the King of the Jews. Their search led them to Bethlehem, where they found the King proclaimed by that brilliant light.

Although these men were Gentiles, the Bible tells us that these astrologers followed the star to worship the newborn King. They had likely spent a long time studying the stars in anticipation of seeing the one that announced the Messiah, and as soon as they saw its light, they traveled a long distance to pay their homage. Their devotion and determination to worship the Savior are reflected in their journey, teaching us the approach we should take throughout this season: the pursuit of truth and genuine worship for the King of our lives.

During this time of year, the preparations, gatherings, and countless other seasonal activities fiercely compete with the light of the star that is Christ for us.

Advent serves as a reminder that we must strive to keep in sight and follow Christ's light, even amid the busyness and distractions of the season.

It is beautiful that God used a star to draw the magi's attention because that was what they knew. It was their field of study; they were interested in and studied the stars. As a ministry, we concluded that God's purpose in revealing Himself to them in this way was to meet them where they were. And God continues to do the same with us. He speaks to us in familiar and meaningful ways to connect with and guide us on our journey towards Him.

The story of the magi is a reminder that God cares for each of us in a personal and significant way and that He meets us where we are.

In these days, as we anticipate the celebration of Christ's birth, let us be watchful. His star will shine amid what we know to capture our attention. And if we follow His light, we will find Jesus in what is familiar to us and even in the everyday routines of our lives.

If we follow the star and resist the temptation to give in to the busyness of the season, we will be guided to true worship and exaltation of our Savior.

All nations will come to your light;
mighty kings will come to see your radiance.
Isaiah 60:3

Create Room for Hope: A Time to Reflect

*In what ways do you feel that God communicates
with you personally and meaningfully?*

How does He guide you on your journey towards Him?

*In what way might God be revealing the light of Jesus in the midst of
what you know, to illuminate your heart and guide you to worship Him?*

*Amid the busyness and distractions of the Christmas season, what can
you do to add intention to your journey as you follow the star this
season?*

*I will instruct you and teach you in the way
you should go; I will guide you with My eye.*
Psalm 32:8

Day 14

When Herod the king heard this,
he was troubled, and all Jerusalem with him.

Matthew 2:3

Day 14

COUNTERCULTURAL WORSHIP

For Christians, worshiping the birth of Jesus stands in stark contrast to the surrounding culture. Imagine, for a moment, the light of the star atop your Christmas tree while all the other lights in your home are turned off. This imagery represents the worship of believers in our society—a beacon of light shining in cultural darkness.

During the Christmas season, millions worldwide engage in some form of worship rooted in their traditions and beliefs. However, authentic worship of the Savior is countercultural, challenging the norms of society. Often, worshiping God is tolerated as long as it doesn't disrupt traditional festivities or alter established methods of celebration.

Today's verse may be brief, but it imparts a profound lesson. When the magi expressed their desire to worship, Herod and all the people were troubled. Do you notice something similar in our current world? As believers seek to worship Christ during this season, popular culture often rises to oppose it. Have you ever wondered why this occurs?

The struggle against true worship began when the season's focus shifted, displacing Christ from Christmas in favor of Santa Claus, decorations, lights, gift exchanges, and presents under the tree.

The commemoration of Christ's birth has been overshadowed by what the culture deems more important. Most alarmingly, we are not exempt from this shift. If we do not stand firm against this pervasive influence, we risk succumbing to cultural pressure and becoming indifferent to genuine worship.

In today's culture, any acknowledgment of God as King provokes resistance. Many respond with hostility, citing injustice, the imposition of religion, and a loss of freedom. Yet, the truth is that worshiping Christ is not a threat but a reminder that His coming is near—a reality that the world fears to confront.

As Christians, we are called to shine our light in the darkness. In a world filled with "Herods" troubled by the worship of Christ, we must, like the magi, resolve to ignore popular opinion, rejoice with great joy, and lift our voices in the worship that our Savior deserves.

God is Spirit, and those who worship Him
must worship in spirit and truth.
John 4:24

Create Room for Hope: A Time to Reflect

Matthew 5:14 says, "You are the light of the world."
How is your worship shining a light for others?

Take a moment to reflect on your worship and celebration practices.
In what ways do individualism and consumerism
tend to overshadow our worship?

How does your worship differ from what is promoted
by popular culture and society?

Is your worship aligned with the truth of the Word,
even if it means standing apart from the crowd?

And do not be conformed to this world,
but be transformed by the renewing of your mind,
that you may prove what is that good
and acceptable and perfect will of God.
Romans 12:2

Day 15

When they saw the star, they rejoiced with
exceedingly great joy. And when they had come into
the house, they saw the young Child with Mary
His mother, and fell down and worshiped Him.
And when they had opened their treasures,
they presented gifts to Him:
gold, frankincense, and myrrh.

Matthew 2:10-11

Day 15

VALUABLE GIFTS

In ancient times, especially in the lands of the East, it was customary for people to present gifts when approaching royalty or someone of importance. Thus, the wise men who sought the newborn King of the Jews spared no expense in their offerings. Their gifts were not just gifts; they brought gold, frankincense, and myrrh—symbols of admiration and reverence.

Could you allow me to explain their symbolism? Gold was a gift reserved for kings, and with this offering, the magi declared the royalty of Jesus. Frankincense was used in Jewish culture as an offering to God, acknowledging the divinity of Jesus. Myrrh, utilized for embalming corpses, foreshadowed their anticipation of His redemptive death for humanity, as foretold in the Scriptures. Beyond their monetary value, these gifts were precious for what they represented.

The Christmas season provides us with an opportunity to give valuable gifts to Jesus. However, to do so wisely, as the magi did, we must first consider how important Jesus is to us personally. These Gentile magi demonstrated with their gifts who this child king represented, not only to the Jews but also to themselves.

Take a moment to contemplate this: Who is Jesus to you? Is He merely the King of the Jews, or is He also the King of your heart? Is He worthy of valuable gifts filled with symbolism, or would a mere trinket suffice to fulfill your religious duty? This Christmas season, will we offer mere material gifts or sincere expressions of our recognition of who He is?

Our gift to the King and Savior of the world should not be a mere obligation, like when we visit friends and make a stop along the way to avoid arriving empty-handed. It should be a gift of contemplation, worship, and closeness as we reflect on His initial arrival to save humanity.

In my own life, I have received a variety of gifts over the years. Some are so valuable that they have left a lasting impression and hold profound significance in my daily life. Some even serve as reminders of the truth of the Word and the disciplines by which I must guide my life. Just as gifts from others are meaningful to us, the gifts we offer to Jesus carry deep weight.

This Advent season invites us to be more mindful as we choose the gifts we bring to the most important person of all—our King and Savior.

For where your treasure is,
there your heart will be also
Matthew 6:21

Create Room for Hope: A Time to Reflect

In light of your personal relationship with Christ,
what symbolic gifts can you offer Jesus this Advent season?

How might dedicating moments to prayer, assisting those in need, and
sharing the gospel serve as meaningful gifts that highlight His
significance in your life in the middle of the season's celebrations?

In what ways do you believe these symbolic gifts can deepen your
connection with Christ during this special season?

Therefore by Him let us continually
offer the sacrifice of praise to God, that is,
the fruit of our lips, giving thanks to His name.
But do not forget to do good and to share,
for with such sacrifices God is well pleased.
Hebrews 13:15-16

Day 16

The Spirit of the Lord God is upon Me,
Because the Lord has anointed Me
To preach good tidings to the poor;
He has sent Me to heal the brokenhearted,
To proclaim liberty to the captives,
And the opening of the prison to those
who are bound.

Isaiah 61:1

Day 16

HARMONY BETWEEN
BROKENNESS AND HOPE

Have you felt a sense of brokenness during this Advent season? I must admit that I often experience this feeling during the Christmas season. It wasn't until recently that I understood why. I used to attribute my brokenness to being unable to gather with loved ones, the busyness of the season, the expectations of others, and the awareness of those who have much less than me. I felt pain knowing that others might be unable to put food on their tables, let alone gifts under their trees. While these reasons still sadden me, I recently realized that my experiences of anguish during the holiday season run more profound than these surface-level concerns.

My brokenness during this season is an expression of the understanding that none of the natural things in this world brought by the Christmas season, despite how joyful they may be, will fill me or provide me with the hope that comes from the birth of Christ. Celebrations, shopping, gifts, and family gatherings often overshadow this profound truth. And so, my spirit groans in brokenness, reminding me that I must cling to true peace and hope in a time when the natural often overshadows the spiritual.

The Christmas season tends to draw our hearts toward festive celebrations. While these moments are enjoyable, the reality is that Christmas is indeed a season for the brokenhearted.

Brokenness allows us to celebrate the birth of Christ by recognizing the hope He brings to our troubled souls. We must acknowledge that we are broken and imperfect beings needing salvation. I've come to understand that if we feel broken during this season, it's a sign that we are celebrating Christmas correctly. Our brokenness and our hope in Him help us understand that without His birth, hope for us would be unthinkable.

Brokenness transforms the holiday season into a profound sigh of anticipation for redemption—the kind that brings life. It reminds us that the birth of Jesus enables us to look forward and live for something far more significant than opening gifts, attending parties, or even the absence of those things. And while our spirits groan, we can find joy and peace through the Holy Spirit, for we abound in hope in a Messiah who came to redeem our wretched souls.

🌿 Are you feeling brokenhearted this season?

Do not feel guilt for it; instead, acknowledge and process your emotions. Please do not suppress it, apologize for it, or try to explain it away. Your brokenness is a spiritual cry that recognizes and celebrates the Savior's arrival. I invite you this Advent season to embrace your brokenness as your soul recognizes its need for the eternal and let your spirit groan in celebration of the birth of Christ. This season is one of genuine hope and peace for the brokenhearted.

The Lord is close to the brokenhearted
and saves those who are crushed in spirit.
Psalm 34:18

Create Room for Hope: A Time to Reflect

*How does your brokenness during the Christmas season
affect your focus on celebrating the birth of Christ?*

*How can you transform your brokenness into a genuine expression of
celebration by understanding that, thanks to Christ, we find redemption
and hope amid our emotions?*

*How can you seek balance by recognizing and processing your emotions
while keeping in mind that true peace and hope come from something
more significant than the temporary circumstances of the season?*

May the God of hope fill you with all joy and peace
as you trust in him, so that you may overflow with
hope by the power of the Holy Spirit.
ROMANS 15:13

Day 17

*In those days and at that time I will raise up a
righteous descendant from King David's line.
He will do what is just and right throughout
the land. In that day Judah will be saved,
and Jerusalem will live in safety.
And this will be its name:
'The Lord Is Our Righteousness.'*

Jeremiah 33:15 - 16

Day 17

JESUS: THE RIGHTEOUS BRANCH OF THE SOUL

Every year, as December approaches, as if the clock of my soul is synchronized with the calendar, I experience a slight desperation for the year's ending. A countdown presses my emotions, longing for New Year's Eve when the midnight mark will allow me to press the reset button on my soul, renewing all my goals, agenda, and priorities. This desire to restart stems from the hope of releasing the weight accumulated over the year that has gradually worn me down.

During the Advent season, while I eagerly anticipate the new beginning that comes with the end of each year, I find in the birth of Christ an encouraging reminder. Jeremiah reminds me that Jesus embodies the renewal I long for each year.

Jesus alleviates the burden of the past year and saves my soul, providing security and righteousness that my midnight reset will never offer. His birth triggers a Righteous Branch, which provides a constant and progressive restoration that brings strength and balance to our lives.

Contemplate the promise of this Branch: "In His days, Judah will be saved, and Israel will dwell in safety." Isn't that what we seek in our desire for a soul reset?

Jesus is the assurance that, amidst life's storms, we can rely on and anticipate complete renewal and salvation daily. He represents that midnight moment, allowing us a continual reset—today, tomorrow, and always—helping us navigate our inner struggles and aligning our agendas.

This Advent, I encourage you to embrace the promise of renewal that comes with the birth of Christ rather than waiting for the New Year's Eve countdown. Please look beyond simply changing the calendar; you can seek genuine and daily renewal in the Righteous Branch. Let the hope that His birth brought inspire you to pursue ongoing spiritual transformation, freeing you from past burdens and leading you into a prosperous new year with the grace and hope that only He can provide.

May this Advent season serve as your reset—a time when your mind, emotions, and worries experience renewal in the radiant light of the Righteous Branch, who is Christ.

But those who trust in the Lord will find new strength. They will soar high on wings like eagles. They will run and not grow weary. They will walk and not faint.
Isaiah 40:31

Create Room for Hope: A Time to Reflect

*What areas of your life do you feel have drained
your energy over the past year?*

In which parts of your life do you sense a deep need for renewal?

*Can you identify specific promises of renewal in the
Bible that have been fulfilled in Christ for these areas?*

Because of the Lord's great love we are not
consumed, for his compassions never fail.
They are new every morning;
great is your faithfulness.
Lamentations 3:22-23

Day 18

"For I know the plans I have for you," declares the Lord, "plans to prosper you and not to harm you, plans to give you hope and a future."

Jeremiah 29:11

Day 18

PLANS FOR ETERNITY

Learning to trust in God and His wonderful plan for my life is a daily journey. Some days, I walk this path filled with joy and peace; other times, I have to push myself to overcome the obstacles, difficulties, and trials that come with carrying my daily cross.

Today, as I reflect on the words of the prophet Jeremiah found in Jeremiah 29:11, I am reminded of their profound significance within their historical context. Jeremiah declared these words during a time of weeping and great uncertainty for the people of God. I encourage you to read the entire chapter of Jeremiah 29. You will discover that God instructed the Israelites to build houses, marry, and also give their children in marriage, to plant vineyards, and seek the city's welfare amidst the difficult circumstances they were living through.

This journey was destined to be long and challenging, but it would not be fruitless. God promised that, despite their trials, He had plans for peace, hope, and a future for them as a nation.

While my experiences in this life may never compare to the seventy years of captivity and suffering endured by the Israelites, I must admit that there are times when my journey feels just as challenging and lengthy. Yet, I find refuge in the hope that, like the Israelites, my journey in this world is not without purpose.

Christmas serves as a potent reminder that God fulfilled His promise to Israel. His covenant with His people came to its fulfillment in the birth of Christ. Jesus, the Savior who would bring peace, hope, and a future to the Israelites, was born just as God had promised. And now, this promise extends to each of us today. By coming to know Jesus and allowing Him to govern our lives, we can build, plant, and move forward on our journey, confident that there are also plans for peace and a beautiful future awaiting.

As we walk through this Advent season, let us root ourselves in the truth that no matter how many obstacles or trials we encounter along the way, or how long our journey may feel, peace, hope, and a better future are always in God's thoughts for you and me. His plan transcends our earthly voyage; it is eternal and carries the promise of everlasting life with Him.

From eternity to eternity I am God.
No one can snatch anyone out of my hand.
No one can undo what I have done.
Isaiah 43:13

Create Room for Hope: A Time to Reflect

Some, like Abraham, did not see the fulfillment of this promise during their days on earth, but we know that this did not mean God's plans would not be accomplished.
In what areas of your life do you need to remember the promise that God has a plan of peace and hope for you?

How can you be more intentional in trusting God's eternal plans for your life, even when you cannot see them right now?

In what ways has faith in God influenced your decisions to build, plant, and move forward on your spiritual journey?

O Lord my God, you have performed many wonders for us. Your plans for us are too numerous to list.
Psalm 40:5

Day 19

But I count my life of no value to myself,
so that I may finish my course and the ministry
I received from the Lord Jesus,
to testify to the gospel of God's grace.

Acts 20:24

Day 19

TRANSCENDENT GIFTS

Have you bought all your Christmas gifts? I imagine you might still have a few left on your list, but before you head out shopping, let me suggest a gift that doesn't require a trip to the store. First, consider this: what do you do with the redemption and grace God has given you? Do you keep them as private memories of personal moments or even as secrets hidden in shame? Let me share a story.

In a season of weakness, my life felt like a dead-end, with my faith fractured and my heart full of questions. Broken and wandering aimlessly, I felt enveloped in darkness, with no glimmer of salvation. I read the Scriptures, but they seemed distant and incomprehensible; my prayers, empty of faith, were little more than whispers that faded away. Accusing thoughts filled my mind, taunting me with the notion that redemption was beyond my reach.

Then, God gave me an invaluable gift: His grace through a friend's story of redemption. Hearing how Christ's redemption transformed a life much like mine became a balm for my soul. I saw evidence of God's joy, peace, and restoration in her, and it filled me with unshakable hope.

I began to believe that redemption was still possible for me and that my shame could be lifted.

Since that day, I've understood that the most meaningful gifts can't be purchased. A story of redemption, born of tears and wrapped in prayer, was the perfect gift that guided me on my restoration journey.

Sharing your own redemptive story, being a testament to God's healing, and allowing others to see His grace at work in your life is a gift that can't be matched.

This Christmas, I encourage you to consider your story of redemption as a gift for someone else. Telling others how Jesus' grace transformed your life could be the most significant present you offer this season. So, set up a coffee date with a friend, a loved one, or someone who's just beginning their faith journey. Share your transformation journey with Jesus and be a living testament to His grace. Let others find encouragement and hope in what you have overcome. Who knows? Your story might change someone's life, just as my friend did for me.

This season, may your story of redemption be the transcendent gift that brings the light of Jesus' hope and grace into someone else's darkness.

Has the Lord redeemed you? Then speak out!
Tell others he has redeemed you from your enemies.
Psalm 107:2

Create Room for Hope: A Time to Reflect

Have you ever shared your story of transformation with someone?
Which part of your redemption story would you
like to give as a gift this season?

Think of someone in your circle who might benefit from
hearing your redemption story.
How could you share your experience with them in a meaningful way?

For I am not ashamed of the gospel of Christ,
for it is the power of God to salvation
for everyone who believes.
ROMANS 1:16

Day 20

He was despised and rejected by mankind,
a man of suffering, and familiar with pain.
Like one from whom people hide their faces
he was despised, and we held him in low esteem.

Isaiah 53:3

Day 20

NIGHT OF GLORY AND SUFFERING

I wish I could say that Christmas is solely about joyful feelings, beautiful decorations, and the glow of bright lights, as our culture encourages us to embrace this during the season. However, the serene Christmas scene and the little child in the manger depict a night that marked the beginning of a story that extends far beyond happy sentiments. Our Christmas narrative is filled with the anticipation of a life of suffering for the Jesus born in Bethlehem.

When sharing the birth story, we tend to emphasize the joy and the light of the star guiding the way to Jesus, often overlooking the profound pain that accompanied it. This inclination may stem from our instinct to seek an escape from suffering—a widespread desire in today's culture. The mantra "Do only what makes you happy" has become a prevailing trend, inviting us to flee from pain in our personal worlds.

The truth is, the Christmas story is a paradoxical blend of joy and sorrow, triumph and sacrifice. In the birth of Christ, we witness the arrival of divinity into humanity, which undoubtedly brings immense joy, but this entrance came at a cost.

The very hands that shaped the stars illuminating the path to Bethlehem were destined to be pierced; the same child who breathed life into humanity would one day cry out in agony as He faced death for humans' sins.

Yet it is precisely in this juxtaposition of pain and glory that the actual depth of Christmas is revealed. The Christmas scene extends beyond the manger to a rugged cross, demonstrating an immeasurable love that willingly embraced all of humanity. Jesus, the incarnation of divinity, voluntarily walked through a valley of suffering so that through His death, we might have the hope of eternity.

As we celebrate Christmas, let us not shy away from acknowledging the pain woven into the story. This very pain magnifies the beauty of the redemptive love that descended that night. By embracing the entirety of the narrative, we discover a love that does not evade suffering or seek mere happiness.

The deeper meaning of the Christmas story goes beyond festivities and bright moments. Let Christ's willingness to suffer for us guide us to embrace our suffering—not as a sign that the world is against us, but as an opportunity to share what He endured for us.

The Father loves me because I sacrifice my life so I may take it back again. No one can take my life from me. I sacrifice it voluntarily.
John 10:17-18

Create Room for Hope: A Time to Reflect

In what ways does culture influence your pursuit of happiness and your avoidance of suffering?

How does acknowledging both joy and suffering in Christ's story change your perspective on Christmas?

In what ways might the interplay of pain and glory in the Christmas narrative deepen the significance of challenging moments in your life?

No discipline seems pleasant at the time,
but painful. Later on, however, it produces
a harvest of righteousness and peace
for those who have been trained by it.
Hebrews 12:11

Day 21

But what things were gain to me, these I have counted loss for Christ. Yet indeed I also count all things loss for the excellence of the knowledge of Christ Jesus my Lord, for whom I have suffered the loss of all things, and count them as rubbish, that I may gain Christ and be found in Him, not having my own righteousness, which is from the law, but that which is through faith in Christ, the righteousness which is from God by faith.

Philippians 3:7 - 9

Day 21

HUSTLE OR ETERNITY?

Christmas Eve is fast approaching, isn't it? Can you feel the holiday bustle that characterizes our culture? The rush to buy last-minute gifts, the pressure to meet expectations, and the stress of preparing for a perfect Christmas Eve—decorating the tree, selecting the right outfit, preparing the food, and countless other details. This flurry can be exhausting, but astonishingly, it doesn't have to be.

Often, the hustle that accompanies the days leading up to Christmas becomes a distraction that overshadows the true reason for our celebration. Resisting the urge to conform and not feeling obligated to ride the wave of cultural currents can make all the difference in our Christmas experience.

Cultural traditions of this season and our insatiable society will always attempt to replace peace with anxiety, joy with disappointment, and worship with indifference. While society may view these exchanges as the norm for the season, I assure you they are not.

The noise of the festive season poses a threat to our true worship. The hustle and traditional demands aim to divert our attention from the Savior, preventing Him from being glorified.

As Christmas Day draws near, be intentional about where your thoughts lie, where your heart leads, and to whom or what you dedicate your time. If our to-do list occupies all our mental and emotional space, we might end up with all the gifts under the tree we think we need, extravagant feasts, and yet lose the joy of celebrating Jesus' birth in our hearts.

Embrace these last days of the season by allowing the hope of eternity to take precedence over the moments of hustle. Could you let it guide your actions?

As Philippians 3:7-9 reminds us, let us count as loss anything that distracts us from Christ's love. Let us renounce worldly concerns and focus on what truly matters: that Christmas finds us in Him. Remember, He is the reason we celebrate and thus deserves to occupy the most significant portion of our attention

Then you will experience God's peace,
which exceeds anything we can understand.
His peace will guard your hearts and
minds as you live in Christ Jesus.
Philippians 4:7

Create Room for Hope: A Time to Reflect

As Christmas Eve approaches, how can you be more intentional about avoiding the hustle and bustle that culture and traditions encourage during this season?

Take a look at your schedule and to-do list:
Is there room set aside for spending more time with Jesus in the coming days? And if not, are you willing to make that adjustment? Even if it means that someone might not receive a gift or that a dish might be omitted from the Christmas dinner table.

Since, then, you have been raised with Christ, set
your hearts on things above, where Christ is, seated
at the right hand of God. Set your minds on things
above, not on earthly things.
Colossians 3:1-2

Day 22

God wants these great riches of the hidden truth to be made known to the people who are not Jews. The secret is this: Christ in you brings hope of all the great things to come.

Colossians 1:27

Day 22

FROM BETHLEHEM TO OUR OWN STABLE

Two thousand twenty-three years ago, in the humble town of Bethlehem, the physical birth of Jesus filled the hearts of those who recognized His arrival as King and Messiah with awe and hope. That night, unforgettable for Mary and Joseph, left an indelible mark on the lives of those who witnessed and adored Him.

I can imagine how each of those people paused long after to reflect on that sacred night. They gathered in homes to recount and relive the excitement of seeing the newborn Savior for the first time and how His presence changed history forever.

Similarly, Jesus was born in our hearts the day we accepted Him as Lord and Savior. Do you remember that moment? I believe you would agree with me that His birth in your heart is as memorable and unforgettable as it was for those who witnessed His physical arrival.

Personally, I still remember what I wore that day as I walked to church, unaware of the birth that was about to change my story forever.

As if it happened yesterday, I recall my tears and those of my friend Marlenne, who, knowing Him well, was filled with joy and took my hand, walking with me to the altar as a witness to my decision to profess Christ's birth in my heart.

The Christmas season serves
as a poignant reminder that, one day,
the birth of Jesus occurred in the stable of our hearts.

Perhaps your conversion was a long preparation process for the Messiah to find a home within you. For years, months, or weeks, you may have been readying your stable for the day He would come to dwell in your heart. Or maybe He arrived unexpectedly, birthing hope when you needed it most. Regardless of how it happened, remembering the moment of His birth in our lives and how it changed our history is the most meaningful way to celebrate this season.

I would encourage you to reflect with gratitude and awe on the day Jesus was born in your heart. Let it fill you with hope as you prepare to celebrate His coming. His marvelous works in our past assure us of His more excellent plans for our future.

And this is eternal life, that they may know You,
the only true God, and Jesus Christ
whom You have sent.
John 17:3

Create Room for Hope: A Time to Reflect

Reflect on the moment Jesus was born in your life.
Where were you? What was that experience like?
Who were you then, and who are you now?

How did His presence change your story?
Do you have any traditions or practices that help you
remember and reflect on His personal birth in your life?

How can you prepare to celebrate with hope
for the return of Christ to earth?

Then Christ will make his home in your hearts as
you trust in him. Your roots will grow down into
God's love and keep you strong.
Ephesians 3:17

Day 23

Then Joseph her husband, being a just man, and not wanting to make her a public example, was minded to put her away secretly. But while he thought about these things, behold, an angel of the Lord appeared to him in a dream, saying, "Joseph, son of David, do not be afraid to take to you Mary your wife, for that which is conceived in her is of the Holy Spirit. And she will bring forth a Son, and you shall call His name Jesus, for He will save His people from their sins." So all this was done that it might be fulfilled which was spoken by the Lord through the prophet, saying "Behold, the virgin shall be with child, and bear a Son, and they shall call His name Immanuel," which is translated, "God with us." Then Joseph, being aroused from sleep, did as the angel of the Lord commanded him and took to him his wife.

Matthew 1: 19 - 25.

Day 23

FROM DOUBT TO OBEDIENCE

Today, we will focus our attention on Joseph, the earthly father of Jesus. Although he was not Jesus' biological father, this fact can sometimes cause his character to fade into the background of the Nativity story. Yet, God chose Joseph for a crucial role in the birth of His Son, and his story is filled with deep emotions and challenges.

The book of Matthew tells us that Joseph was a righteous and faithful man, a descendant of David who was betrothed to Mary. I imagine him as a young man filled with hopes and plans, about to marry the woman of his dreams, utterly unaware of the upheaval that lay ahead in his life.

When Mary received the announcement of her pregnancy with the Son of God, maybe filled with doubt and fear, she decided to visit her cousin, Elizabeth, for three months. Meanwhile, Joseph waited for her, and it was only upon her return that she revealed her pregnant condition. Can you imagine Joseph's surprise, feelings, and inner conflicts that wrapped within his soul at such news? The confusion, distrust, and anguish that must have enveloped him?

The woman he loved was pregnant, and he was not the father. The explanation for this pregnancy was quite questionable. I can't blame him for considering leaving Mary in those moments; it must have felt like his world had come crashing down.

Without a doubt, Joseph's faith was being tested, yet amid his uncertainty, he believed the angel's voice. He didn't need to know how, why, or what the future held for them. He chose to submit his faith to the divine instruction and not to leave his betrothed. He remained and married Mary. I greatly admire his trust in God's instructions amidst such uncertainty.

Joseph's obedience was indeed a challenge. It meant accepting the unknown and facing criticism and questions from others. However, despite everything, Joseph seemed to understand that his story was not about him. His obedience became a provision for the protection Mary and Jesus needed to fulfill God's plan. What a significant role Joseph played in the story!

Joseph teaches us that faithful obedience means trusting in God's message, His works, and His lordship, even when doubts and circumstances are bewildering.

Not everyone who says to Me, 'Lord, Lord,'
shall enter the kingdom of heaven, but he who
does the will of My Father in heaven.
Matthew 7:21

Create Room for Hope: A Time to Reflect

Is there something that God is asking you to do that feels challenging? How can you demonstrate obedience like Joseph's in response to His command?

To what extent do you believe Joseph's obedience affected the divine plan for the birth of Jesus?

How can Joseph's faith in divine instructions inspire you in your own life?

Then Jesus said to his disciples, "If any of you wants to be my follower, you must give up your own way, take up your cross, and follow me." Matthew 16:24

Day 24

But when the fullness of the time had come, God sent forth His Son, born of a woman, born under the law, to redeem those who were under the law, that we might receive the adoption as sons. And because you are sons, God has sent forth the Spirit of His Son into your hearts, crying out, "Abba, Father!" Therefore you are no longer a slave but a son, and if a son, then an heir of God through Christ.

Galatians 4:4-7

Day 24

CHRISTMAS EVE: ABOUT TO BE ADOPTED

I have never experienced the adoption of children firsthand, but I have met people who have. I've also seen touching videos on social media that depict tears of joy, overwhelming emotions, and heartwarming stories behind adoptions. Hopeful parents eagerly anticipate the moment they can bring a child home to care for and love as their own. Children are speechless and have tear-streaked faces when they hear that someone loves them enough to provide them a home—someone they can now call Mom and Dad.

Christmas Eve is, in essence, the preamble to our adoption story. You and I were like orphans, lost in sin, separated from God, and without a home. We needed shelter, care, and someone we could call Abba. Then, Christ came to our rescue and took us as his own.

This Christmas Eve, we are immersed in an adoption story where we are the protagonists, the children being adopted.

Adoption became an eternal reality for us in the form of a baby Messiah, born in a manger, granting us a home that can never be taken away. An "Abba" and father to whom we can confidently run, and an inheritance in heavenly places. What more could we desire? It is a perfect adoption story. The love of God demonstrated in the gift of Jesus, is the most significant and cherished adoption narrative we will ever know.

This Christmas Eve, as we anticipate commemorating the initial arrival of the Savior, let us remember our divine adoption with gratitude for our redemption and joy as we wait for a future beyond compare.

Tonight is a good Christmas Eve because it is the anticipation of the birth of the One who loved us enough to leave His throne and come to earth to secure for us an eternal future. He came to redeem us forever, to love us unconditionally, to guide us into truth, and to bring us home at His second coming.

But as many as received Him, to them He gave
the right to become children of God,
to those who believe in His name
John 1:12

Create Room for Hope: A Time to Reflect

Have you ever had personal experiences where you felt the need for a spiritual home or divine care, similar to the adoption story?

Reflect on this profound truth: through Christ, the supreme God and creator of the universe has made you His child and invites you to a close relationship with Him as your "Abba."
Can you feel the significance of your own adoption story?

Those who are victorious will inherit all this, and I will be their God and they will be my children.
Revelations 21:7

Day 25

*Today in the town of David
a Savior has been born to you;
he is the Messiah, the Lord.*

Luke 2:11

Day 25

CHRIST: THE SUPREME GIFT

'Christ is the greatest gift of all'—a phrase we hear so often on Christmas Day that it can almost sound like a cliché. For centuries, it's been used to express the blessing He brings to the world and the joy of salvation that came through Him. Yet, for some, the words might feel distant, like a beautiful package that hasn't been unwrapped.

So, how do we unwrap this incredible gift? How do we experience its fullness when it's something intangible? When His promises aren't immediately visible? Or when the joy behind this declaration feels far from our current reality?

I've seen children and adults alike unwrap gifts under the tree with eager excitement, only to feel a pang of disappointment because it wasn't what they wanted or expected. Perhaps today, you, too, received a gift that didn't quite meet your heart's desire, leaving a trace of letdown. Just like that, unrealistic expectations can dull the thrill of unwrapping the gift of salvation. It is hard to experience the fullness of joy at the sight of humanity's supreme gift when we do not fully grasp its true significance in our personal lives.

The gift of salvation is our supreme gift, not because it's what we expect but because it's what we need. Jesus is the gift we each desperately need! Without Him, there is no hope, no life, no future. But with Him, and in Him, there is salvation, fullness, abundance, and eternity!

Christ is the gift that transcends the tangibles of life's sufferings and challenging circumstances. The gift of Jesus grants us an unshakeable peace anchored in the hope that He will return one day, and tears will be wiped away, our circumstances will be redeemed, and we will have eternal joy and peace once and for all.

Unwrapping the gift of salvation is something we can do every day. We do this by reflecting on all His birth has accomplished for us: salvation, redemption, freedom, grace, favor, and eternal hope. Today, besides all these, can you see the other gifts His birth has brought into your life?

For me, one gift stands out as incredibly supreme and precious: the understanding and freedom that cannot be taken from me. His birth placed the keys to my prison in my hands. Now, it's up to me to choose whether I live in that freedom or remain bound.

May this Christmas, and each day after, be filled with the joy of unwrapping the gift of Christ's presence in your life.

¡Thanks be to God for his indescribable gift!
2 Corinthians 9:15

Merry Christmas!

As this Advent season draws to a close, I pray that you've taken to heart one or two precious truths about how Jesus' salvation has given us eternal hope, joy, and fullness that no tradition or culture could provide. His return for His church is hope everlasting —the promise that one day, we will dwell with Him for all eternity. As you wait for His return, hold on to this truth: in Him, so long as we remain grounded in faith, we can unwrap the gift of His grace each day, anchored in the eternal hope He offers us, one promise at a time.

How will you keep unwrapping the gift of Christ's salvation after this Christmas day?

Anchor your hope in the eternity that awaits in Him!

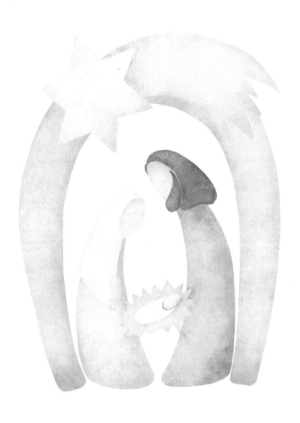

*And the Word became flesh and dwelt among us,
and we beheld His glory, the glory as of the only
begotten of the Father, full of grace and truth.*
John 1:14

WHAT COMES AFTER ADVENT?

Dear Reader,

Stay Alert! While our journey through this devotional has ended, a question remains: how will we respond to this experience? Not only does what we did during this season matter but what we choose to do from here on will keep our faith anchored in the hope of eternity.

Advent is more than an annual celebration; it's a reminder that we are awaiting our Savior's return and that our hope can be kept alive because of that promise. Here are three simple yet powerful ways to carry our hope forward:

- Share the Good News with others! Jesus came to save all of us, and His love is meant to be shared. Who in your life needs to experience this hope? Constantly take a moment to pray for an opportunity to share His love with those around you, knowing that your words can be a light in their lives.

- Keep your hope alive through God's Word. The Bible is a treasure of divine truth and wisdom. Dive into Scripture, study the life and teachings of Jesus, and find strength in God's promises. His Word is an anchor for your soul, holding you steady through life's storms. Counter the lies that culture, the world, and the enemy whisper into your ears with the truths within God's Word.

Invite the Holy Spirit to transform you. True holiness doesn't come by our strength but through the Holy Spirit's power. Allow Him to search your heart, purify your spirit, and prepare you for Jesus's return. This is how we grow closer to becoming the vessels God has designed us to be.

Remember, you are part of the story of redemption! Keep hope alive, and be a source of inspiration to others as we await our Savior's glorious return.

May God bless you and guide you as you step forward with faith, anchored in the eternal hope we share.

In His Love and Hope,
Waleska Cruz, CEO
Disciplinas Libertadoras Ministiries

When everything is ready, I will come and get you, so that you will always be with me where I am.
John 14:3

Connect with the Author

Connect with Fani and follow her writings through Disciplinas Libertadoras Ministry.

https://www.facebook.com/disciplinaslibertadoras

@fanireyes-dejesus

A call to women to embrace freedom in Christ,
and to silence the lies of the enemy with the truth of the Word,
One Discipline at a Time.

Scripture. Transparency. Judgment-Free Zone. We Meet You Where You Are.

FIND US ON SOCIAL MEDIA

 @disciplinaslibertadoras

#disciplinaslibertadoras
#unadisciplinaalavez
#SomosDL

Do you want to cultivate biblical disciplines for your daily life in practical ways?

Available in English and Spanish.

Order your copy today of the Bible Study and Disciplines Journal through Disciplinas Libertadoras' Ministry.

https://www.facebook.com/disciplinaslibertadoras

Would you like to receive free resources from Disciplinas Libertadoras' Ministry?

Disciplinas Libertadoras Ministry offers a variety of free resources to help you develop spiritual disciplines for your daily walk with Christ.

- Scripture Cards
- Articles and Writings
- Pre-recorded Programs
- Community
- And more!

By using our resources alongside the Scriptures, you will find **redemption**, **freedom**, and **fullness** to live without reproach,

One Discipline at a Time!

You can request our resources through our Facebook and Instagram pages or by sending an email to **somosdl@disciplinaslibertadoras.com**

Made in the USA
Columbia, SC
19 November 2024